DIY

create, design, reinvent, and make it yours!

Planet

Yumthing

Do-It-Yourself

Ela Jaynes and Darren Greenblatt

Line drawings by Darren Greenblatt

bantam books

new york • toronto • london • sydney • auckland

Published by
Bantam Books
an imprint of
Random House Children's Books
a division of Random House, Inc.
New York

Visit us on the Web! www.randomhouse.com/teens
Educators and librarians, for a variety of teaching tools, visit us at
www.randomhouse.com/teachers

ISBN: 0-553-37595-4

The text of this book is set in 12-point Agenda Medium.
Book design by Angela Carlino

Printed in the United States of America

February 2004

10 9 8 7 6 5 4 3 2 1

Welcome to the world of Planet Yumthing,

your one-stop do-it-yourself destination dedicated to making the life around you hip and totally your own. We are best friends, obsessed style-watchers, and pop-culture junkies, and we want to help you make your world a better, sassier place. And we've come up with a bunch of original projects that can help you do just that. They are easy to make *and* easy on the wallet. *Planet Yumthing DIY* deals with what's relevant and important to you: fashion, beauty, your own personal space, and hanging with your friends.

You want to change your old jeans into a skirt? Revamp your room into a modern retreat? Recharge your body with a homemade tootsie soak? Or throw a luau? This step-by-step guide will not only tell you what supplies you'll need to make it all happen, but it will also guide you through the process.

You don't have to go very far to find your own personal style. Some of the most inspiring things are cluttering your closet right now. Coolness is definitely not just bought straight off the rack. The world is your canvas, and you can paint it exactly the way you envision it.

In the world of Planet Yumthing, there is no right or wrong. If *you* like the way something turns out, that's what's important! If you mess up, or get stumped along the way, take a deep breath and try again (we certainly did when we were making these projects for the first time). Don't forget, it's not all about the end result: it's also about having a good time getting there!

Grab your friends, roll up your sleeves, and get started!

XOXO

Ela Jaynes + Janen Greenblatt

The Planet Yumthing Manifesto

- We believe change is good.

- We believe you should trust your instincts.

- We believe you shouldn't chase every trend . . . otherwise you'll be a fashion victim.

- We believe you can be whatever you want to be *before* you grow up.

- We believe crafts don't have to be corny.

- We believe the world around you is really just a free art supply store.

- We believe your room is your kingdom.

- We believe not in *what* you wear but in *how* you wear it.

- We believe style equals power.

- We believe in public transportation.

- We believe in old mixed with new.

- We believe in colors that don't match.

- We believe in colors that magically belong together.

- We believe you get what you settle for.

- We believe your friends are more interesting than movie stars.

- We believe you should be interest*ed* and interest*ing*.

- We believe in making it rather than buying it.

- We believe in collecting things *and* letting things go.

- We believe you should surround yourself with what you love.

- We believe if you make a mistake, you can learn more than if you did it perfectly the first time.

- We believe if you mess up, you should try again.

[Contents]

[Chapter 1]

DIY Fashion 1

[Chapter 2]

Beauty, Body & Soul 25

[Chapter 3]

Your Space 43

[Chapter 4]

Food, Fun, and Friends 65

[Chapter 1]

DIY Fashion

**Unleash the inner fashion designer in you
by turning your old duds into genuine diva wear.**

Alterna-Skirts

Deconstructed Jeans Skirt

Digging in your closet for a hot new skirt to wear? Use the wrong side of denim to patch one together!

You will need:

- A pair of jeans
- Fabric scissors
- A seam ripper (Get one at a fabric store.)
- Straight pins
- A strong needle and colorful coat or embroidery thread
- A thimble

How to:

1. Cut the legs off your jeans just below the knees. Hold on to these pant legs for later.

2. Use the seam ripper to split open the inseam on each leg of your cropped jeans. In the front, rip the seam up to the zipper. In the back, rip the 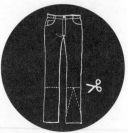 seam up to the yoke, the seam just above the back pockets. Get rid of loose threads, but don't worry about the raw edges.

3. Using the sketch as a guide, fold the seams that you've just cut so they overlap and lie smooth. Pin the fabric down with straight pins so the jeans lie smooth.

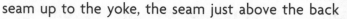

4. You'll now see what looks like a skirt with phantom triangle pieces missing in the front and back.

5. Grab those leftover pant legs. Cut along one seam of each leg so you have two rectangular pieces of fabric to work with.

6. Cut two triangles out of the pant legs that are about 1 inch bigger all around than the triangular spaces you want to fill.

7. Place one fabric triangle with the wrong side up under one side of the skirt to fill in the triangular space. Move the fabric around until it lies flat and fills in *all* the space. Pin this piece securely in place with lots of straight pins.

8. Do the same thing for the other side of your skirt, making sure to place the triangular piece wrong side up. You can always try on the skirt (watch those pins!) to see if the triangles are in the right spots.

9. Sew down the folded seams (from step 3) and sew the triangular pieces to the skirt. Try using a different color thread. If your stitches aren't perfect, don't worry. It'll just look cool.

10. If you need to, even out the hem of your skirt with scissors. After you put your skirt in the wash, the edges of the cuts you made will rag out just the way you like it.

11. Use the seam ripper to carefully remove the skirt's front coin pocket and the back pockets to reveal cool dark detailing where the pockets used to be.

 It helps to use a thimble when you sew through the thick layers.

Alterna-Skirts
Rock 'n' Roll Skirt

Inspired by old concert tees, this is a great way to show support for your favorite band—without looking like all the other groupies.

You will need:

- An oversized rock concert tee. The fit should be big and long.
- Fabric scissors
- A needle and thread
- A large safety pin
- Multicolored plastic beads

How to:

1. Turn your tee inside out. Cut straight across the shirt just under the armholes. You will be left with a tube (aka your skirt).

2. Cut a 1-inch-wide strip of fabric off the bottom of the tube. This long, skinny strip will become the drawstring for your skirt.

3. Fold back 1 ½ inches at the top of the skirt and sew around it approximately 1 inch down from the folded edge. The tube you create at the top of the skirt is your waistband!

4. Turn the skirt right side out again. In the center front of the waistband, cut a vertical slash ¾ inch high.

5. Pin the large safety pin to one end of the drawstring and thread the drawstring through the waistband.

6. Try the skirt on to decide the length. Cut the bottom straight across or on a diagonal.

7. To make fringe, cut vertical slashes 1 inch apart around the bottom hem of your skirt. Tug on the fringe to make it roll up and get skinnier.

8. Slide the colored beads onto the fringe and make a knot at the end of the fringe to hold them in place.

Alterna-Skirts
Beach Towel Mini

Terry cloth feels soft next to your skin. So make a miniskirt out of an old beach towel and head for the nearest pool!

You will need:

- A large beach towel (It should be big enough to wrap around your body 1 ½ times. Or you can buy terry cloth at a fabric store.)
- Safety pins
- A washable marker
- Fabric scissors
- Two 1-inch squares of Velcro
- A needle and thread
- Pom-pom trim (optional)

How to:

1. Wrap the towel around you so it sits smoothly on your hips.

2. Use the safety pins to pin the corners of the towel together.

3. While the towel is still wrapped around you, use a washable marker to mark X's in between the flaps of towel, where the safety pins are. To do this, make two X's on the underside of the top flap of towel. Then make two X's on the topside of the bottom flap of towel, for a total of four X's. Don't worry if you make a mark in the wrong place; the ink will disappear in the wash!

4. Separate the Velcro. Unwrap your skirt and use the safety pins to pin the 1-inch squares of Velcro onto the X's. Pin fuzzy-sided Velcro to the 2 X's on one end of the towel and scratchy-sided Velcro to the 2 X's on the other side of the towel. (When the towel is folded around your waist, they should stick to each other.)

5. Sew the Velcro onto the towel. Cut your skirt as short as you dare. For fun, sew pom-pom trim around the bottom of your new mini.

Alterna-Skirts

Back-to-School Ballerina

Wear this easy-to-whip-up tulle skirt over jeans and pair it with a T-shirt for school . . . or wear it over a slip or skirt for Friday night fun.

You will need:

- 6 yards of tulle
- 2 to 3 yards of wide ribbon (long enough to tie around your waist with a bow)
- Chalk
- A large yarn or embroidery needle
- Acrylic yarn
- Fabric scissors
- A sewing needle and thread

How to:

1. Fold the tulle in half lengthwise. Hold it horizontally.

2. Tie the ribbon tightly around your waist with a bow. With chalk, make marks on the ribbon on either side of the bow. This lets you know how big your waistband will need to be.

3. Thread the yarn needle, but do not cut the yarn.

4. While the yarn is still attached to the skein, sew long (about 1-inch) stitches 1 inch down from the folded edge of the tulle.

5. While you're sewing, you can begin to gather and scrunch the material across the yarn (think of curtains on a rod). Be gentle—you don't want the yarn to rip.

6. When you're finished sewing, push the fabric together so it's the

same length as the markings you made on the ribbon. When you hold the skirt up to you, it should wrap comfortably around your waist. If not, adjust the fabric.

7. Cut the yarn and tie knots in both ends, making sure you haven't changed the size of the waistband while you are knotting.

8. Lay the ribbon on top of the yarn stitches, lining up the chalk marks with the edges of the skirt. Sew the ribbon onto the tulle with a regular needle and thread.

9. Trim the extra tulle above the ribbon with scissors. Cut the skirt to whatever length you want.

 Tulle comes in many varieties. Choose tulle with larger netting holes instead of delicate tulle. You can use more or less yardage, depending on your size or how poufy you want your skirt to be. The more yards, the more pouf.

 Experiment with layers of tulle. Try aqua tulle over navy. Black tulle over hot pink. Cut the bottom unevenly so the second color peeks out!

 Use polka-dotted ribbon and save a little extra to make a choker!

 Our friend Pauley, who's in a rockin' girl band, sewed tiny fake flowers onto the tulle. She wears hers over jeans with a baseball tee and her fave tennies.

Designer Tees

Pin It!

Show your punk-rock edge. Rock stars have nothing on you when you sport this slashed and pinned tee with leather pants or your favorite pair of low-riders.

You will need:

- A tight, long-sleeved crew neck T-shirt
- Fabric scissors
- Safety pins in various sizes (and lots of 'em)

How to:

1. Cut 4 inches off the end of each sleeve.

2. Use your scissors to slash the tops of each sleeve up to the shoulder seam.

3. Cut a long V-shaped slash in the center front of the neck.

4. Use pins to pin together all the slashes. Decide how tight you want to re-pin the shirt. Experiment with different-sized pins.

 You can slash and cut even more places on the tee and then pin them back together.

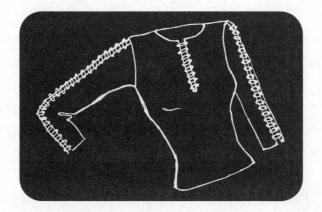

Designer Tees

Pull It!

We've seen these sassy and sweet tops in boutiques for way too much money. When you see how easy it is to make one, you'll agree.

You will need:

- A T-shirt (One that fits you well works best.)
- 1 yard of 1-inch-wide ribbon
- Fabric scissors
- A needle and thread
- 24 inches of silk or leather cord in a contrasting color
- A safety pin

How to:

1. Turn your tee inside out.

2. Cut 4 strips of ribbon, each 5 inches long.

3. Sew a strip of ribbon at each side of one of the tee's side seams. To do this, sew a line of stitches on either side of the ribbon close to the edges. You will be creating a tube that a cord can pass through.

4. Pin a small safety pin to the cord and thread it up one tube, then out and back down the second tube. Leave extra cord so you have enough to tie in a bow.

5. Repeat on the other side of the tee.

6. Tie the ends of your cord in a knot.

7. Turn your tee right side out. When you put it on, cinch the fabric along the cord and hold it in place by tying a bow. Be daring—pull the sides up to different heights!

Designer Tees

Stencil It!

Say what you feel! Paint your own logo tee that represents who you are or what you feel. Sweet. Naughty. Fresh. Brainy.

You will need:

- A T-shirt
- Cardboard
- Fabric paint
- Sponge paintbrushes
- Stencil letters (homemade or store-bought)
- Masking tape
- An X-ACTO knife
- An old magazine
- A pencil

How to:

1. Lay the shirt flat. Slide a piece of cardboard inside the shirt so paint can't seep through.

2. Paint a wide horizontal stripe across the chest of the shirt. Make sure there isn't too much paint on the brush (it's better to do multiple thin coats over dry paint than to glob on tons of paint the first time).

3. When the paint stripe is dry, lay the stencil letters down on the stripe exactly where you want them to be. Use masking tape to hold the stencils in place.

4. With a second color, dab a thin layer of paint over the stencils. Remember, use a little paint at a time, adding layers as needed after each color dries.

To make your own stencil:

You will need some thin cardboard, an X-ACTO knife, an old magazine, and a pencil. Draw your design or words in block letters on a scrap piece of paper first to get the shape right. Make sure you make connector spaces (where lines cross each other) in your design on the cardboard so the letters will look right when you cut them out. Practice with your scrap paper, coloring in where you would cut. When you're satisfied, draw the design on the cardboard and cut it out with the X-ACTO knife, using a magazine as a cutting board.

Painting Tips

 The sponge brush should be clean and dry before starting each paint color.

 Allow paint on the T-shirt to dry fully between coats of different color. This way colors won't bleed.

 Don't worry if the stenciling or the paint job isn't perfect. (You can always say you meant it to be that way, right?)

PYT It!

 Check out some of our all-time fave color combos: chocolate brown stripe/deep red letters/powder blue tee . . . black stripe/ metallic silver letters/red tank . . . red stripe/fluorescent pink letters/black tee

Designer Tees

Stud It!

Feeling rock 'n' roll but with a prep-school wardrobe? Follow these directions and make your own rock star tee.

You will need:
• A piece of paper
• A ruler
• A pen
• A solid-color tee
• Rhinestones
• Rhinestone settings
• A coin

How to:
1. On a piece of paper, draw a word that describes you. Get cool! Get crazy! Get funky! Just make sure the word is not too big for the front of your tee.

2. Use the ruler and a pen to mark dots on the design at equal intervals up to an inch apart, depending on how many rhinestones you have.

3. Place the paper on top of your tee. With your pen, mark the dots through the paper onto the tee.

4. Put a rhinestone faceup into a rhinestone setting. Place the rhinestone and setting on a marked dot and poke the prongs through the fabric of the tee.

5. Holding the rhinestone in place with your fingers so it doesn't slip out of the setting, use the coin to fold the prongs down on the inside of your tee.

6. Repeat steps 4 and 5 until all the dots on your tee are covered with shiny rhinestones!

If you have a cute logo tee that needs a little dazzle, just follow steps 4 and 5, using the existing logo as your guide. You can use a contrasting-color rhinestone to trim the sleeves or neck.

Cigar-Box Purse

Luckily, you don't need to be a cigar puffer to make this adorable and classy purse. If you don't have a stogie-smoking uncle, just stop by the nearest cigar shop and ask them for a leftover box.

You will need:

- A cigar box
- Fine-grade sandpaper
- Measuring tape
- Scissors
- Fabric pieces big enough to cover the bottom of the box (try upholstery fabric from a fabric store's scrap bin)
- Rubber cement
- 1 yard of decorative braid or trim (¼ inch wide)
- A handle (available at many craft stores) or thick rope (from a hardware store)

How to:

1. Sand the inside of the box to smooth any rough edges. Wipe out loose dust.

2. Measure the inside bottom of your box. Then cut a square or rectangular piece of fabric to fit. You can also do the same for the top of the box.

3. Glue the bottom piece of fabric inside the box and smooth it down. Do the same for the inside lid.

4. Glue the decorative trim or braid around the edges of the fabric to cover or finish the raw edge.

5. If you use a handle from a craft or specialty trims store, decide where you would like to place it. Some boxes work better on their side, because of their shape.

6. If you use thick rope, ask your local hardware store if they can drill two holes in the top of your box. Have them make the holes 4 inches apart and centered on the top of the box, just large enough for the rope to fit through. Poke the rope through both holes to form a handle. Cut the rope after you tie knots on the inside of the box, so the rope handle can't slip through the holes.

Finishing Touches

- *Tie small decorative tassels to the handle.*
- *Screw feet or "rests" into the bottom.*
- *Glue a tiny mirror to the inside lid.*

Denim Bum Bag

Made from the seat of an old pair of jeans, this bag is a great way to put last year's denim to excellent use. You can also try this one with old cords or khakis.

You will need:

- An old pair of jeans
- Straight pins
- Fabric scissors
- Coat thread or embroidery floss
- A strong needle
- A thimble
- 1-inch-wide Velcro
- A sewing machine (optional)

How to:

1. Button your jeans, keeping the zipper un-zipped.

2. With your jeans lying flat, line up the front and back waistbands so they are lying on top of each other. Pin them in place with a few straight pins.

3. Cut the legs off your jeans 1 or 2 inches below the zipper. Don't worry if you cut through the front pockets. You should have what *looks* like a super-duper miniskirt.

4. Cut off all the belt loops.

5. Remove the pins from the waistband and turn the whole thing inside out.

6. Sew a straight line across the bottom. If you're sewing by hand, make sure your stitches are close together. This will be the bottom of your bag, and you don't want stuff to fall out later.

7. Unbutton the jeans. Carefully cut off the waistband so you have one long piece to use as a strap.

8. To make the closure, cut a piece of Velcro that is as long as the *width* of your jeans. Separate the Velcro and sew one piece to the front and one to the back on the inside of the jeans, at the top edge. Velcro (especially the scratchy side) can have a mind of its own. It always helps to pin even the smallest piece of Velcro down before sewing it on. It also helps to stitch through the edges of the Velcro so the scratchy part doesn't rip your thread.

9. To finish the shoulder strap, turn your jeans/purse right side out again. Using sturdy, strong stitches, sew the old waistband to either side of the bag on top of the side seams. You can make your straps shorter or longer, depending on where you place them before sewing them down.

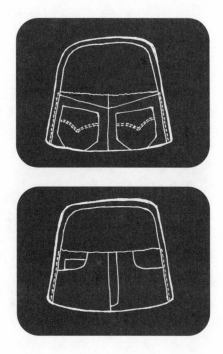

Curtain-Panel Sundress

Sometimes all the inspiration you need is hanging right in front of you! Check out these easy directions for a summer dress made from inexpensive window treatments.

You will need:

- A curtain panel with loops. Find one at a discount megastore (try sheer panels with a little texture).
- Fabric scissors
- 3 yards of decorative ribbon—long enough to tie a bow around your waist
- A needle and thread
- Pinking shears

How to:

1. The loops at the top of the curtain panel will become the straps of your dress. You will need four loops. Wrap the panel so it fits around your body with a little give around the hips. Line up four loops (two in front and two in back) where you'd like them to fall on your shoulders.

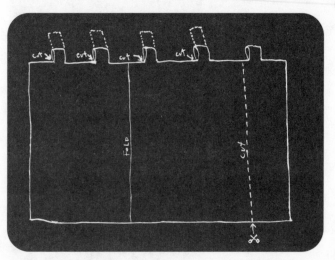

2. Lay the panels flat. Fold the portion of the fabric with the four loops/straps in half, with the good side of the fabric on the inside. Line up the straps on top of each other.

3. Using the sketch as a guide, cut away the rest of the curtain panel. Cut off any extra loops besides the four you need.

4. With the dress still inside out, sew the side of the dress closed. Don't sew all the way down to the bottom of the skirt—this way you'll have a sassy side slit in your dress.

5. Cut one end of each loop (on the inside of the dress, at the base of the loop) to create a long strap. Right side out, try your dress on and tie the straps so the dress hangs where you want it.

6. To give your dress a cute baby-doll fit, cut ½-inch slits every 2 inches around the dress, below your bustline (in other words, in between your belly button and bust). Weave a ribbon in and out of the holes, starting and ending at the front center of the dress. Cinch and tie it in a bow.

7. Cut the hem of your dress with pinking shears for a decorative edge.

Use extra material to make cute shoulder bows!

Tie-Dyed Slip Dress

With a few supplies and a washing machine, you can turn an old thrift-store slip into a Near Eastern–inspired dress with sunset hues and colorful accents.

You will need:

- A needle and thread
- A white or pastel full slip
- Fabric dye
- A washing machine
- Salt
- Multicolored paillettes (colorful metallic disks available at a fabric or craft store)
- Rubber bands

How to:

1. Wrap three rubber bands tightly around the bottom of the slip, spacing them about 2 inches apart. This will prepare the slip for a striped tie-dyed pattern.

2. Next, you want to prepare for rosette patterns around the body of the slip. Grab small bunches of fabric between two fingers and tie a couple of rubber bands around them. Make more of these bunches and rubber-band them, randomly spacing them around the front and back of the slip.

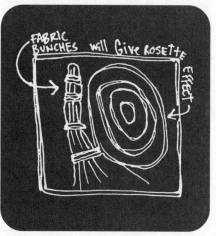

FABRIC BUNCHES will Give ROSETTE EFFECT

3. Read all the directions and warnings on the fabric dye before starting.

Turn the washing machine settings to small load, hot/warm cycle and let it fill with hot water. Carefully add the fabric dye to the water.

4. Pour 1 cup of salt into the washer.

5. Once the dye has completely dissolved and is evenly dispersed in the water, put the rubber-banded slip into the machine for the remainder of the wash cycle. (If you want, throw in some white socks or underwear that you want dyed too!)

6. When the cycle has ended, remove the rubber bands. Hang the slip to dry, or put it in the dryer. After you're done, run the washing machine on cold with nothing in it to rinse out any excess dye. When washing your new slip dress, wash it alone or with like colors in cold water.

7. For the finishing touch, sew paillettes to the center of each rosette for a glam sari look!

 Slips that are 100% cotton will dye differently than slips made from synthetic material like polyester. Cotton will dye darker and truer to the color on the box. Synthetic fibers don't take dye as well; they'll turn out more muted, with a dustier hue than the color on the box.

 If you want your dress to turn out two-toned, dye the entire slip in a paler color before you rubber-band it. Let it dry. Rubber-band the slip and dye it a second time in a darker color.

PYT Picks

Think of the color of sunsets, like tangerine orange, crimson, aquamarine, and royal blue.

Starlet Cardigan Redo

Jazz up a cardigan Hollywood-starlet style, complete with ¾ sleeves and rhinestone trim.

You will need:

- A cardigan
- Fabric scissors
- Measuring tape
- A 1-inch-wide ribbon of your choice (Velvet is easy to work with.)
- Straight pins
- An iron
- A needle and thread
- Rhinestone buttons or rhinestones

How to:

1. Cut the sleeves to ¾ length (3 to 5 inches below your elbow) for a 1950s look.

2. You will need to edge the bottom of the sleeves with ribbon so they won't unravel. To do this, measure the new wrist hole you've just cut. Cut a piece of ribbon that measures the total of that length, plus ½ inch extra.

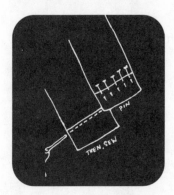

3. Fold the ribbon in half lengthwise, securing it with straight pins. Iron the fold to create a stiff crease.

4. Sandwich the end of the sweater's sleeves with the folded ribbon. Pin the folded ribbon to the sweater all the way around. Make sure you catch both sides of the ribbon with the pins.

5. Hand-sew the ribbon to the sweater about ¼ inch in from the unfolded edge of the ribbon. Again, make sure that while you're sewing, you're catching all layers of fabric (the two sides of the ribbon and the sweater).

6. When you're done with both sleeves (and if you're feeling ambitious), repeat the edging process with the bottom hem of your sweater.

7. Snip off the old buttons and replace them with rhinestone buttons from a vintage or fabric store. Or, even easier, hot-glue rhinestones on top of flat buttons and let them dry overnight.

Quickie Redo

Many fabric stores sell binding—fabric ribbon that is already folded. If you're planning a bunch of cardigan redos, this can be helpful!

Insider Info!

Keep your eyes peeled for inexpensive clothes in vintage and thrift stores that have way-cool buttons. Sometimes it's worth buying something just for the buttons.

Designer Tip

To measure something that's round or curved, try measuring it with a piece of string or ribbon first. Then lay the string on a ruler to get the exact measurement . . . perfect every time!

PYT It!

We found a vintage red cardigan and added leopard-print ribbon and black rhinestones for instant va-va-va-voom!

[Chapter 2]

Beauty, Body & Soul

Making your own beauty products doesn't mean
you have to build your own chem lab. You can use
natural ingredients to make simple recipes that
refresh and restore your body and skin.

Aromatic Tea Bag Bath Packs

Create your own bath time tea bags and steep your body in invigorating scents.

You will need:

- ½ cup of fresh herbs or flower petals or ¼ cup of dried herbs or flowers
- 2 tablespoons of oatmeal
- Coffee filters
- String

How to:

Make a bunch at a time! Place herbs or flowers and oatmeal in the middle of a coffee filter. Cinch the filter closed with string and tie it in a knot. Cut the string long enough that you can tie it around the tub spout. Steep the tea bag under the spout with hot water while filling the tub. Leave the tea bag in the water while you take your bath.

- *Try rose petals and lavender when you're feeling romantic.*
- *Mint is soothing after a workout.*
- *Soak with chamomile to relax your mind . . . perfect for the night before exams.*

Design your own gift tags and attach them to the string (they'll look like real tea bags). Put a few bath packs in a basket, throw in a CD you've burned, and voilà—insta-present!

Berry Beautiful Mask

This aromatic mask can help your skin look and feel softer while helping to clear up minor blemishes.

You will need:

- 1 cup of fresh strawberries
- 1 tablespoon of water
- 2 tablespoons of cornstarch
- 2 tablespoons of milk

How to:

1. Remove the stems from the strawberries, then wash and slice them.

2. Mix all the ingredients and mash them into a paste.

3. Spread the mixture over your face and neck (bath time is perfect). Keep the mask away from your eyes.

4. Relax with your eyes closed for 20 minutes.

5. Rinse with warm water, splash with cool water, and pat your face dry.

6. Any leftovers? Your mask mixture will keep in the refrigerator as long as the milk is fresh.

 This mask smells great—enjoy the scent and take slow, deep breaths while you relax.

Pear Facial Mask

Pears are an excellent source of sorbitol, a natural sugar that acts as a humectant (it helps keep your skin moisturized). This yummy recipe is a great soother for sun-drenched skin or skin with some blotches and redness.

You will need:
(enough for one mask)
- 1 *ripe* pear
- 1 tablespoon of honey
- 1 tablespoon of light cream or whole milk

How to:
1. Peel and core the pear and cut it into small pieces.

2. In a small bowl, mash the pear into a smooth paste.

3. Stir in the honey and cream.

4. Spread the mixture over your face and neck. Keep the mask away from your eyes.

5. Relax with your eyes closed for 20 minutes.

6. Rinse with warm water, splash with cool water, and pat your face dry.

 Did you know that using milk or cream to keep the skin milky-smooth is an old Southern beauty trick?

Honey-Vanilla Bath and Tootsie Soak

This total body treat will make your skin feel silky and smooth, while the honey and vanilla create an oh-so-heavenly scent that lingers long after your bath.

You will need:

- ½ cup of unscented mineral or baby oil
- ½ cup of honey
- ½ cup of unscented liquid soap
- 1 tablespoon of vanilla extract
- A squeeze bottle (A honey-bear bottle is perfect and looks cute in the bathroom!)

How to:

Mix all the ingredients so the honey dissolves, and pour into the squeeze bottle. Shake the mixture a little before pouring it into the bath. Use about ¼ cup for a bath . . . and a few squirts for a foot soak.

Nourishing Face Salsa

The combo of carrot (high in beta-carotene and antioxidant vitamins), cream (high in calcium and protein), and avocado (loads of vitamin E) makes for a deliciously moisturizing mask that can help improve your skin's texture.

You will need:
- 1 carrot
- 1 avocado
- ½ cup of heavy cream
- 3 tablespoons of honey

How to:
1. Fill a saucepan with water, add the carrot, and boil until the carrot is soft. Drain, cool, and mash to a paste in a bowl.
2. Cut the avocado in half. Remove the pit and scoop the meat into the bowl with the carrot. Mash the avocado and carrot together.
3. Add the cream and honey and mix well.
4. Spread the mixture over your face. Avoid your eyes! Leave it on for 15 minutes.
5. Rinse with cool water and pat your face dry.

 This mask feels thick and funky. Just remember Ela's grandma's words of wisdom: the thicker the mask, the more intense its natural powers.

 If you're in the bath with your mask, use the cleaned avocado pit as a natural massage tool by rolling it over your feet, legs, and arms!

Oatmeal Smoother

This facial cleanser contains ground oatmeal, a natural exfoliator that helps remove dead skin cells and absorbs surface dirt. Yogurt softens skin, and honey (as you may have noticed) serves as an amazing humectant, helping to lock moisture into the skin.

You will need:

- ½ cup of oatmeal
- 2 tablespoons of honey
- ¼ cup of plain yogurt

How to:

1. Mash and gently grind the oatmeal with the back of a spoon to break up the oats.

2. In a small bowl, mix the oatmeal, honey, and yogurt into a paste.

3. Smooth the paste over your face and neck with a gentle, circular motion. Avoid your eyes! Leave it on for 15 minutes.

4. Rinse with warm water and pat your face dry.

Rosy-Glow Astringent

Rose petals and water make a very simple, natural cleanser.

You will need:

- 1 cup of fresh rose petals
- 1 cup of distilled water
- A small bottle

How to:

1. Place the petals in a bowl. Set it aside.

2. Bring the distilled water to a boil, then pour it slowly over the petals.

3. Steep for 30 minutes.

4. Strain the petals and pour the rose water into a small bottle.

5. Store the astringent in the fridge and apply it with cotton balls.

 Make sure the rose petals you use are pesticide-free. Your best bet? Pick your own roses from a reputable source or from a rural, untended rosebush.

 The rose petals will impart a beautiful color to your astringent. Try using only one color of rose for each astringent you make; each one will have a different hue. Label astringent with the rose's hybrid name for a romantic beauty treat.

School Daze Apple Toner

Apple-picking season is a great time to make this after-school pick-me-up! Not only are apples great to eat (they're loaded with potassium and vitamins A and C), but they can also refresh your skin. This beauty treat works well for all skin types.

You will need:

- 1 apple
- ³⁄₄ cup of water
- ¼ cup of witch hazel
- A small jar or spray bottle

How to:

1. Core and chop the apple into small pieces. You don't need to peel it.

2. Put the apple chunks and water in a small saucepan. Bring to a boil, then remove it from the heat.

3. Let the mixture cool, then strain it, letting the juice run into a bowl filled with the witch hazel.

4. Stir gently and pour the mixture into a small spray bottle or jar. Apply it with cotton balls, or store in the fridge for a cooling after-school spritz!

 Red apples will make your toner a pretty pink.

 When Darren was little, his family would go to Styers Orchard in Bucks County, Pennsylvania, where he learned a lot about the natural benefits of apples.

DIY Labels

It's groovy to make your own beauty products . . . but why stop
there? Feel like a pro by making your own labels for your creations.
They make cool gifts and will also look great in your own bathroom.

You will need:

- Cardboard
- Decorative paper
- Ribbon or twine
- Rubber cement
- Scissors, or, even better, pinking
  shears for that cute zigzag edge!

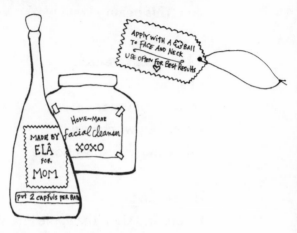

Labeling Tips

Make your own logo. Think of a word that represents you or a mood
you want to evoke (like sporty or Zen or chill). Draw a symbol or letter
the word decoratively to represent the sentiment. Use this logo on
each label.

Think about colors and what they mean: let the colors you choose represent the vibe of your beauty line. Name your beauty concoctions
with fun names like Moonbeam Massage Oil or Bedtime Bath Soak. If
they're a gifts for a friend, personalize the beauty treats with the
friend's name.

A great gift-giving idea: Pack bottles neatly in a small box. Just before
giving the gift, sprinkle flower petals over the bottles. Spritz with per-
fume before sealing. Don't forget to include instructions and the list of
ingredients.

Zen Out

It's a hectic world out there. It is totally important to take some time out for yourself. Aromatherapy can turn your bedroom or bathroom into a cozy and relaxing haven.

Aromatherapy 101

Aromatherapy is the use of essential oils to lift your spirits and make you feel good. Essential oils are highly concentrated extracts derived from plants. They contain properties and fragrances that when used externally are thought to help heal or soothe the body and mind. Sometimes it's the fragrance itself that helps, and sometimes vitamins or healing properties within the extract are responsible for helping to make you feel better. You can find essential oils at health food, herbal, or homeopathic stores. If you have an allergic reaction or experience any kind of skin irritation, stop using the oils immediately. If the problem persists, see a doctor.

Spa Essentials

As you experiment with essential oils, try these basic recipes. They can turn a boring bath time routine into your own spa experience. Using Aromatherapy Mix and Match as a guide, *you* decide which essential oils to use to create the atmosphere you want!

Bathtub Soak

Dilute 6 drops of essential oil in 2 cups of milk and stir, then pour into a warm running bath.

Foot or Hand Soak

Add 4 drops of essential oil and the juice of ½ a lemon to a small tub of warm water.

Massage Oil

Mix 4 drops of oil for every 2 tablespoons of carrier oil. A carrier oil is an oil base made from olive, jojoba, carrot seed, or almond oil. You can find these at health food stores. When giving a message, focus on the hands and feet (where most of the body's important pressure points are). Massaging pressure points helps to relieve tension all over the body!

Diffuser

This is great to try while meditating, stretching, and practicing yoga, or even when you're daydreaming in your room. You can buy a diffuser that will hold the oils of your choice and sit on top of a lightbulb. When the oil warms up, it scents the air. If you don't have a diffuser, you can make your own (if you don't mind relaxing in the kitchen). Fill a small saucepan with water. Bring the water to a boil. Lower the heat and add 10 or so drops of oil. Let simmer for a few minutes. Then turn off the burner. The scent will linger while the steam is still rising. Always keep an eye on the stove; don't let the water boil away and burn your pot.

Air Freshener

Add 6 drops of essential oil to a small spray bottle filled with water. Mist the fragrance into the air, not directly onto anything.

Aromatherapy Mix and Match

Get to know the different properties of various herbs and flowers.

Chamomile
- Good before bedtime
- Good for calming nerves
- Soothing

Jasmine
- Sensual
- Spirit-lifting
- Stimulating

Juniper
- A good tonic and cleanser
- Good for problem and oily skin

Lavender
- Gentle and calming
- Helps to heal damaged skin

Lemon
- A natural astringent
- A natural deodorizer
- Helps to strengthen the immune system
- Refreshing

Lemongrass
- A disinfectant
- An insect repellent
- A natural deodorizer

Patchouli
- Calming and sensual
- Has decongestant properties

Rose
- Spirit-lifting
- Romantic and highly aromatic

Sandalwood
- Moisturizing
- Soothing and healing
- Spirit-lifting

Ylang-ylang
- Good for stress relief and insomnia
- Spirit-lifting

Mantra Meditation Candles

These soothing candles will remind you to slow down and reflect.

You will need:

- Teacups and saucers
- Multicolored permanent markers
- Paraffin wax or candles
- A double boiler
- Wicking
- Metal wick holders

How to:

1. Start with a clean, dry teacup and saucer.

2. Think of your personal mantra: a sentence or saying that represents words you like to live by. Write this mantra on the rim of the saucer with permanent marker, and on the outside of the teacup if you like.

3. Melt the wax or candles in the top portion of a double boiler.

4. Cut the wicking 1 inch longer than the depth of the teacup.

5. Attach the wick you just cut to a metal wick holder. Place the wick and holder in the center bottom of the teacup.

6. While holding the wick straight up, carefully pour the melted wax into the teacup. Fill the cup ½ inch below the rim.

7. Let the wax cool for at least 1 hour. (The top layer of wax will harden quickly; the middle may still be gooey.)

8. Trim the wick to ½ inch above the candle. To burn a candle safely, always trim the wick to this length before lighting it.

Mix and match the patterns on the cups and saucers. Garage sales are a great place to look for unique designs.

 Try a mini-meditation. Sit comfortably cross-legged on the floor in a dimly lit room. Place the candle in front of you and light it carefully. Breathe slowly and deeply through your nose (rather than your mouth) and think of your mantra. Clear your head of all other thoughts. It's not easy! It takes some practice, even if you're trying to focus for only a few minutes. When you're done, blow out the candle.

 Remember, never leave a hot stove unattended.

Daisy Crown

You don't have to wait for spring to celebrate the flower child inside you!

You will need:

- A bunch of flowers—choose ones with thick stems and hearty blossoms, like multicolored daisies or carnations.
- A knife
- Twist ties

How to:

1. Cut the stems of your flowers so they are 3 inches long.

2. Slice a ½-inch slit in the middle of the stem of the first flower with a knife.

3. Slide the second flower's stem through the slit until the blossom catches.

4. Now slice a ½-inch slit in the middle of the second flower's stem.

5. Slide a third flower's stem through and continue in this way until you have a chain large enough for a crown.

6. You can fasten your crown into a circle by cutting a longer slit in the last flower and sliding the blossom of the first flower through the last flower's stem. Or you can fasten the crown with a ribbon and a bow.

7. Use twist ties to make your crown extra sturdy. Once you've made your crown, wrap the twists once or twice around the stems and trim the excess with scissors.

If the pickings are slim in your backyard, you can use flowers from a grocery store or market to make this oh-so-natural accessory.

 Going to a concert? For that eye-catching touch, get together with your friends before the show and make flower crowns for everyone to wear.

 For a pretty effect, glue tiny rhinestones to some of the petals with a glue gun.

For a pretty effect, glue tiny rhinestones to some of the petals with a glue gun.

Don't forget to give your botanical halo some love by spritzing it with water just before you leave the house.

[Chapter 3]

Your Space

Your room is your castle. That is, it will be, with these crafty ideas for redecorating and organizing.

Poetry Patchwork Sheets

Mix and match sheets patchwork style and give your room a great personalized look.

For a double bed, you will need:

- 1 pillowcase and 1 flat sheet in one color; 1 pillowcase and 1 flat sheet in another color
- A needle and thread
- 6 yards of rickrack
- Fabric scissors
- Straight pins
- A ruler
- Pinking shears
- Fabric paint
- A small paintbrush
- Safety pins

How to make mix 'n' match pillowcases:

1. Cut about 4 inches off the open-ended side of each pillowcase. (You can use the seam that runs along the open end of the pillowcase as a guide.)

2. Sew each onto the other pillowcase.

3. Sew rickrack over the seam to hide it.

How to make a patchwork flat sheet:

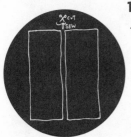

1. Cut both sheets in half lengthwise. Sew one sheet to the opposite sheet half so you have one top sheet that is two-toned. Set aside the other two sheet strips.

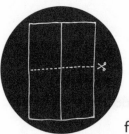

2. Cut the two-toned sheet in half horizontally.

3. Spin one half around and sew the sheet back together so the color patterns are opposite each other, making a four-square patchwork pattern.

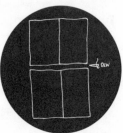

4. Pin rickrack over the seams to hide them. Sew the rickrack down with a needle and thread. Remove the pins.

How to make a poetry-inspired dust ruffle:

1. Measure the distance from the top of your box spring to the floor. Add three inches to that number. This will be the length of your dust ruffle.

2. Use pinking shears to cut strips this width from the sheet pieces you set aside earlier. Sew the strips together, short end to short end, until it's long enough to wrap around the sides of your bed. Alternate the color of fabric if you don't have enough material in one color.

3. Working on cardboard for protection, use fabric paint to write a lyric from your favorite song or a quote you want to live by on this long strip. Fill the entire length of the bed ruffle. Let it dry.

4. Tack the dust ruffle to your box spring with safety pins.

 A sewing machine makes this craft easier—it involves mostly straight lines and easy-to-sew fabric. But you can also do it completely by hand!

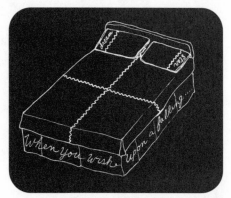

Froufrou Lamp

Turn an ordinary lamp into a statement that will add charm to any bedroom.

You will need:

- A lampshade, new or used
- String
- A pen
- Trim of your choice
- Scissors
- A hot-glue gun
- Postcards (We like vintage black-and-white Hollywood images.)
- Tape

How to:

1. Working with the lampshade removed from the lamp, use string to measure the lampshade by wrapping it around the top and marking the string with a pen. Lay the string next to the trim and cut it the same length as the marked string.

2. Do the same for the bottom of the lampshade.

3. Plug in the hot-glue gun. While it's heating, decide where you want your postcards to go. Use tape to tack the postcards up, moving them around until you're satisfied with their placement.

4. First remove the tape, then glue the postcards to the shade one at a time.

5. Glue the trim to the top and the bottom of the shade. Remember: never let any trim or add-on items touch or get near the lightbulb!

6. If your lamp has a pull cord to turn it on, sew a rhinestone button to the end for a final touch.

Room Tip

 Use low-watt bulbs, like 40 watts. Or try rose, blue, or gold light-bulbs for mood lighting.

 Try thrift stores, or buy an inexpensive shade from a discount store. Plastic shades, not fabric, work best for this project. You can use any lamp base as long as the shade fits. The shade is what gets all the attention!

Fun Options

 Surf-Shack Style: Use raffia trim (available at a craft or a trim-ming store) and beach scene postcards. Or instead of postcards, use vacation stickers.

 Hobo Style: Glue squares of cut fabric haphazardly to the lamp-shade. Don't worry about fraying edges—it's part of the look! Cut craft store felt into fringe and glue it to the bottom of the shade.

Your Bedroom

Room Divider

Create a separate area in your room—who doesn't need that?

For a 6 x 6-foot room divider, you will need:

- Thirty-six 12 x 12-inch squares of cardboard. Start saving cardboard boxes now—don't worry if there's writing on them.
- Acrylic paint
- A paintbrush
- Sponges
- A hole puncher
- A ruler
- A pencil
- Jumbo paper clips (150 should do you just fine.)
- 12 coffee mug hooks (available at a hardware store)
- Ball chain and ball chain closures (sold by the foot at a hardware store) or twine

How to:

1. Make a diagram of your room divider. Decide what design you want and color it in on your diagram. (We made ours with silver chrome, cherry red, and powder blue.) Use the diagram to figure out how many squares of each color you will need to paint.

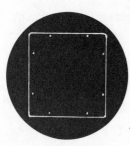

2. Paint the cardboard with two coats so the color is very opaque. Use a sponge for a funky texture. Let it dry.

3. Punch two holes on each of the four sides of one cardboard square. Space the holes 2 inches from each corner and ½ inch in from the edge. This will be your template.

4. Lay the template on top of the rest of the squares and mark the holes with a pencil. Punch the holes where you marked.

5. Using your diagram as a guide, attach the squares with the paper clips.

6. If you're hanging your room divider from the ceiling, have someone help you screw the mug hooks up there. Use the ball chain or twine to hang the room divider from the mug hooks. This way you can decide how high or low you want your divider to hang.

 You can adjust the size of your divider using more or fewer squares (and paper clips!), according to your space.

 For a bohemian look, try using only brown cardboard (without writing), and instead of paper clips, attach the squares with natural-colored twine or string. Glue a dried autumn leaf to the middle of each square.

Cool Trick

 Make a doorway by strategically leaving out squares!

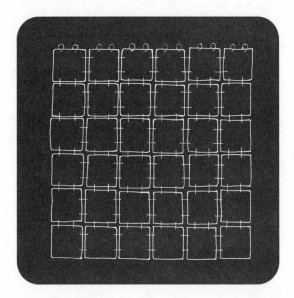

Wacky Clocks

Fabric Pushpin Clock
Chinese Takeout Box Clock

Great gifts. Perfect for your bedroom or your locker. Once you've figured out how to make one, the sky's the limit—any container will work!

You'll need these supplies to make a Fabric Pushpin Clock:

- A piece of craft store felt
- Pinking shears or fabric scissors
- A battery-operated clock movement (from a craft store)
- Duct tape
- Flat Styrofoam
- Silver pushpins

How to:

1. Cut a square or circle of felt.

2. Assemble the clock parts according to the instructions on the clock movement package, except instead of inserting a traditional clock face, use your felt.

3. Secure the clock movement to the back of the felt with duct tape.

4. Place the clock faceup on the Styrofoam. This will hold the clock in place until it is put on the wall.

5. Place pushpins to represent numbers around the face of the clock, pushing through the fabric and into the Styrofoam.

6. Install the clock by simply pushing the pushpins into the wall to hold the clock up!

You'll need these supplies to make a Chinese Takeout Box Clock:

- A battery-operated clock movement
- A Chinese food takeout container
- A Chinese takeout menu
- Rubber cement

How to:

1. Follow the package instructions for the clock movement and place it in the middle of the takeout box so the arms of the clock are visible on the largest side of the box.

2. Cut numbers from the takeout menu (or cut letters to spell out the numbers) and glue them in place around the face of the clock!

Other Containers to Use for Wacky Clocks

- *A large tin can with a cool label*
- *A deflated soccer ball*
- *A Frisbee*

Ribbon Memento Board

With this take on the old-fashioned love letter memento boards, display to-do lists, your mail, photos, and generally cool stuff you can't bear to throw away (you know, concert ticket stubs, your secret crush's dropped bubble gum wrapper . . . not!).

You will need:

- 1 piece of ½-inch thick foam core board, 30 x 40 inches (available at art supply stores)
- 1½ yards of fabric (gingham or toile looks pretty)
- A pen
- Scissors
- Spray adhesive (available at craft and art supply stores)
- A stapler
- Straight pins
- 6 yards of ¾-inch ribbon
- A hot-glue gun
- 30 to 36 (medium to large) flat buttons (You can use all one color or mix 'em up with varied vintage buttons.)

How to:

1. Lay the foam core on top of the back side of the fabric. Trace the foam core onto the fabric with light pen marks. Add 2 inches all around with the marker and a ruler.

2. Follow the second markings to cut the fabric out. Follow the directions on the spray adhesive can to attach the fabric to the front of the foam core. Wrap the extra fabric neatly around the back of the foam core. You can use glue or masking tape on the back side to secure the fabric.

3. Using the sketch as a guide, starting at the top right corner and working your way down, cut and pin (with straight pins) the ribbon tautly across the foam core in equally spaced diagonals, 7 inches apart.

4. For the opposite direction, starting at the top left corner, cut and pin ribbon strips 7 inches apart so they form symmetrical diamond shapes with the first set of ribbons you pinned on. To keep the board looking symmetrical, place these ribbons at the same degree of diagonal (or angle) as the first set, but in opposite directions.

5. Open your stapler so you can staple the ribbon to the board. Staple once or twice at the intersections of two ribbons. Make sure the ribbon is pulled tight across the board and lies smooth.

6. Remove all the straight pins.

7. Using a glue gun, glue buttons at each ribbon intersection to strategically cover the staples. Let dry.

8. Hang your memento board using leftover ribbon, stapling the ends securely to the back side of the foam core.

 You can slide lightweight mementos like photos behind the ribbon to hold them in place. Heavier items like letters can be tacked to the board with pushpins.

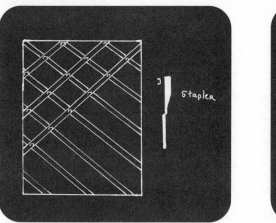

stapler

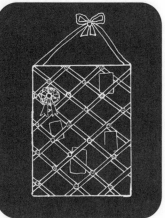

Chichi Shoe Box

Old shoe boxes are great for storing everything from CDs to hair gear.

You will need:

- A shoe box
- A ruler
- A pencil
- Craft paper or newspaper
- Scissors
- Straight pins
- Fabric (Choose a wacky mixture of prints, solids, and stripes.)
- Fabric scissors (Pinking shears work great.)
- Fabric glue
- Grosgrain ribbon

How to:

1. Measure the shoe box (the bottom, not the lid): the length, width, and height.

2. With the sketch as a guide, use your measurements and a ruler to draw a paper pattern on the craft paper or newspaper. Add 2 inches to the edges for what will become flaps. Make sure your right angles are perfect.

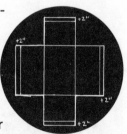

3. Cut out the paper pattern and fold the paper around the box to be sure it fits properly.

4. Lay the paper pattern on top of the wrong side of the fabric and pin it together with straight pins. Try to keep the fabric as smooth as possible while you're pinning.

5. Cut the fabric following the paper pattern. Be careful not to move the fabric while you cut.

6. Now it's time to glue the fabric onto your box. Start by spreading glue on the bottom of the box. Match up the middle of the fabric with the bottom of the box and smooth it down. Move on to one side of the box, spreading glue on the box first and then smoothing the fabric. Put glue onto the extra 2 inches of fabric and fold this extra piece over to the inside of the box. Do the same for the other three sides of the box.

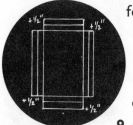

7. Make a pattern for the lid in the same way you did for the bottom of the box. This time you'll need to add an extra ½ inch for the flaps instead of 2 inches.

8. Again, cut the fabric out and glue it to the lid of the box in sections.

9. Cut a 5-inch piece of ribbon. Fold it in half and glue the ends together. Once it has dried, and using the sketch as a guide, glue the folded ribbon to the inside of the lid (on the short side) so it hangs out of the box, acting as a pull.

Designer Tips

To make a bigger statement, make a bunch of boxes. Using the same size shoe boxes will let you reuse your paper pattern.

Mix up patterns for a pro look: plaid bottoms with pinstriped tops . . . think of textured fabrics, such as lightweight corduroy, wool, seersucker—your local fabric store has it all!

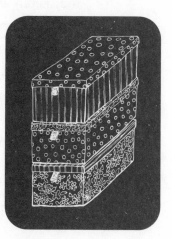

Organize it!

Tin Can Organizer

Keep your supplies together in this cute and kitschy organizer, perfect for holding lightweight items like pens and pencils.

You will need:

- Scrap lumber (something close to a 2 x 4, about 1 foot long)
- Sandpaper
- Acrylic paint
- A paintbrush
- A hammer
- Six 1½-inch nails
- 3 clean tin cans (Select ones that have cool labels: pie filling or colorful salsa cans work nicely.)
- Wire

How to:

1. Use sandpaper to smooth down the edges of the board.

2. Paint the board to complement your tin cans.

3. Cut off or fold down any sharp edges on the tops of the cans.

4. Using the sketch as a guide, nail the first can to the center of the board. To do this, hammer one nail through the opening of the can and into the wood. Hammer the nail close to the top edge of the can. You may have to hammer the nail at a slight diagonal, but try to keep it as level (horizontal) as you can. Hammer the second nail close to the first, also trying to keep it as horizontal as possible.

5. Nail the remaining two cans equidistant from the middle can to the ends of the board.

6. Wrap and twist wire around the ends of the board, leaving enough slack in the middle to hang the organizer on the wall.

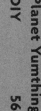

Mementos, Memories, and Keeping in Touch

Vacation Picture Frames

Collecting mementos is a great part of any vacation. But what to do with your finds? Put your treasures on picture frames to bring back a bit of your trip to someone special.

You will need:

- A 5 x 7-inch frame
- Paper
- A pencil
- Collected items such as small shells from the beach or mini-pinecones from the mountains
- A hot-glue gun

How to:

1. Lay the frame on a piece of paper. Trace around the frame onto the paper to create a template.

2. Now lay the mementos or treasures you want to use inside the template lines. This is your chance to see how they'll look.

3. Change the placement so your frame is pleasing to the eye. Bigger pieces look better placed toward the corners and on the bottom.

4. Take each piece off one at a time and glue it to the frame. Continue until the entire frame, including the sides, is covered with your vacation treasures.

5. Pop in a photo of you from your trip!

The trick to making this project look really cute is to go overboard with covering the frames for a three-dimensional effect. Cover the entire surface—the sides and edges—and then glue some more on top of that!

Far-out Postcards

Getting snail mail is always exciting. But writing can sometimes be a drag, so why not make it fun by using alternative stationery? Just keep in mind the regulations of our friends at the United States Postal Service.

Furry Postcards

Cut faux fur into wacky shapes—daisies, stars, and hearts. Cut cardboard into the same shape and glue it to the back.

Googly-eyed and Missing You

Glue googly eyes (available at a craft store) onto a photo of yourself. Draw in a mustache or a bubble quote about how much you miss your friend. Back the photo with cardboard.

Road Trip

When you're on the road with your folks and have all that extra time, cut a road map into rectangles and back them with cardboard or glue them to cheapie postcards. Get thrifty: some cities give out complimentary subway maps and bus maps.

Reduce, Reuse, and Recycle Pop Art

Think about recycling in a new way by cutting cereal boxes into standard postcard-sized rectangles. All you have to do is write on the back, address it, stamp it, and mail it.

Message in a Bottle

Roll up a letter and slide it into a clean plastic soda or sports bottle. Take off the original label completely. Screw the top back on. Tape an index card with the address and appropriate postage on it to the outside of the bottle.

Matchbook Art

Snag matchbooks and business cards from cool restaurants and stores you go to on your trip and glue them onto a rectangular piece of cardboard in a creative collage.

Foreign Labels

When you're in another country or even in another part of the U.S., scout out unusual indigenous food. Look for cans of hominy if you're in the South or scrapple if you're in Pennsylvania. (What is scrapple, anyway?) Carefully peel the labels off and back them with cardboard.

Postal Factoid

A standard postcard measures between 3 ½ x 5 inches and 4 ¼ x 6 inches. Anything sent postcard-style (no envelope) that measures differently or is not rectangular needs first-class, letter-rate postage.

Accordion Photo Album

The best memories deserve a special place. Sure, you can go out and buy any old photo album, but making one from scratch is much better. It's more meaningful and special . . . whether you make it for a friend or to hold your own memories!

You will need:

- 2 pieces of thick cardboard, measuring 9 x 11 ½ inches each
- 2 pieces of decorative paper, measuring 11 x 13 ½ inches each (We used vintage wallpaper. You can also try other printed paper like gift wrap, sheet music, foreign-language newspapers, or beautiful images from a magazine.)
- Spray adhesive
- 8 pieces of 8 ½ x 11-inch black construction paper
- Black tape (available at a craft or art supply store)
- A pencil
- A ruler
- Decorative ribbon (6 pieces cut into 7 inches each)
- Rubber cement

How to:

1. To make the back and front covers of the photo album, place decorative paper over the cardboard. Use spray adhesive to glue it down. Fold the edges of the paper over and glue them neatly to the back of the cardboard.

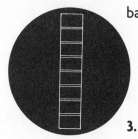

2. To create the album pages, tape two pieces of the black construction paper together, side by side (not overlapping) with a strip of black tape running down the length of the two pieces of paper.

3. Using the sketch as a guide, continue taping the rest of the

black papers together in this way until all the papers are connected by tape. Trim any excess tape off the bottom or top.

4. Fold the paper back and forward on top of itself like an accordion. Put it aside.

5. To mark where you need to put the ribbon closures on the covers, set the two pieces of covered cardboard in front of you with the back sides facing up. On the long side of each cardboard piece, make a mark exactly in the middle of the board and exactly ¼ inch in from the edge.

6. On the other long side of each cardboard piece, make two more marks: both ¼ inch in from the edge, one 2 inches from the top and the other 2 inches from the bottom.

7. Glue ribbon over your marks. You'll need to glue each ribbon 2 inches in from the edge and let the rest dangle.

8. Use spray adhesive or rubber cement to glue the last page of the black accordion pages to the back side of one of the covered cardboard pieces. Smooth the paper with your hands, making sure it's secure. Now all the messy stuff is covered.

9. Do the same with the second piece of cardboard. Glue the first page of the black accordion pages to the back side of the second piece of cardboard. This will become your cover. Before you glue, make sure the cardboard is turned the right way, with the ribbons lining up with the first piece of cardboard.

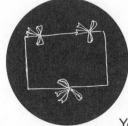

10. When the glue is completely dry, tie the ribbons into double-knotted bows. The side with the two bows will be the spine of your photo book. To open and close the book, use the side with one ribbon.

You're now ready to fill your book with photos. You can tape or glue them in, but the coolest way is to use old-fashioned photo tabs—pick them up at a photo lab or stationery store.

Hidden Treasure Book

Keep ultra-top-secret documents—love notes, your journal—from the grimy hands of your pesky little brother.

You will need:

- An old, thick hardcover book—a used bookstore has plenty
- A pen
- Heavy cardboard
- An X-ACTO knife
- A ruler
- Rubber cement
- A small piece of fabric
- Paper clips

How to:

1. Open the book 20 pages in. Using the sketch as a guide, draw a rectangle in the middle of the right-hand side. Leave a border on all sides.
2. Cut the cardboard in the same size (length and height) as the interior of the book. Measure the rectangle you drew on the page. Draw the same size rectangle onto the cardboard piece. Use the X-ACTO knife and a ruler to cut out this rectangle piece.
3. Starting on page 20, place the cardboard template on the page. Cut out rectangular pieces from the pages by following the template with the X-ACTO knife. You will have cut away several pages at a time. Continue cutting rectangles from the pages until you get to the back cover.
4. Use rubber cement to glue the last page to the back cover. Continue gluing pages together, working from the last page forward to the first page you cut.

5. Cut the fabric to fit inside the hole you've created in the book. Glue the fabric down with rubber cement.

6. Let the book dry with the cover of the book and the first 20 pages open. If you have to, use paper clips to keep them off the rest of the book so they won't accidentally get glued down.

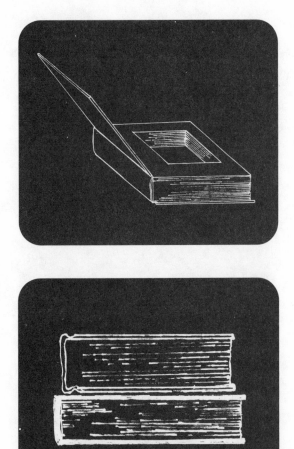

[Chapter 4]

Food, Fun, and Friends

Ho-hum weekends are a thing of the past. Watch your social life soar with these easy-to-plan parties.

Route 66 Truck Stop Party

If cruising across America isn't in the cards, bring the freedom of the road to your house with this outdoor truck stop party.

The Ten-Four, Good Buddy, Vibe

- Use road maps as invitations.
- Set up buckets of water and sponges near the garden hose and driveway. Friends with cars get a free car wash!

Dress Code

- Think of gear that you've seen at truck stops . . . jeans and plaid shirts, mesh-backed baseball hats, cowboy hats, big belt buckles, and vacation tees.
- Bring bathing suits for car wash fun!

Pedal to the Metal Party Favors

- Bargain-basement CDs and kitschy cassette tapes
- Pine-tree air fresheners
- Cheesy bumper stickers
- Smiley-face antenna balls
- Beef jerky sticks

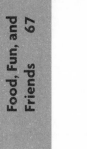

Music

- Patsy Cline
- Dolly Parton
- Elvis (the Graceland years)
- Hank Williams (Jr. and Sr.)

Inspirational Movies

- *Road Trip*
- *Smokey and the Bandit*
- *Cannonball Run* and *Cannonball Run II*
- *Thelma and Louise* (Just don't take it seriously.)

Food Fixin's

- Mac Daddy
- Frito Pie
- Road Hog Root Beer Float
- Aunt Audrey's Ice Cream Pie

Mac Daddy

Can macaroni and cheese be any better than this? No. It can't.

You will need:
- 1 pound of elbow macaroni
- 4 tablespoons of margarine or butter
- ½ cup of all-purpose flour
- 4 cups of milk
- 3 cups of shredded cheddar cheese
- 2 cups of cheese curls or puffs
- A pinch of salt
- A dash of pepper

How to:
1. Boil the macaroni according to the directions on the box. Drain and put it aside.

2. Melt the margarine in a large pot. Be careful not to burn it.

3. Blend in the flour, milk, shredded cheese, and 1 cup of the cheese curls or puffs.

4. Simmer over low heat until the cheese melts.

5. Add the salt and pepper.

6. Add the macaroni to the cheese sauce and mix well with a wooden spoon.

7. Turn off the stove.

8. Pour the cheesy macaroni into a greased casserole.

9. Top with the remaining shredded cheese and cheese curls or puffs.

10. Bake at 350 degrees for 30 minutes, until it's golden brown on top and bubbly.

Frito Pie

Ya like spicy? Ya like crunchy? Ya like gooey cheese and a kick of salsa? Of course ya do!

You will need:

- 1 large bag of Fritos
- 1 large can of chili (veggie or with meat)
- 1 onion, chopped
- 1 can of sliced jalapeño peppers (optional)
- 1 cup of shredded cheese (cheddar or jalapeño jack)
- Sour cream

How to:

1. Pour the corn chips into a pie pan or baking dish. If you're using a microwave, pour them into a microwave-safe dish.

2. Heat the chili, then spoon it over the corn chips. Top with the onions, jalapeños, and cheese.

3. Heat it in the oven (or microwave) until the cheese is melted.

4. Serve it with sour cream on the side.

Road Hog Root Beer Float

Nothing satisfies a thirst and a sweet tooth like this supereasy drink.

You will need:

• Root beer
• Vanilla ice cream
• Tall glasses

How to:

1. Fill ice cube trays with root beer and freeze.

2. Layer the float. Start with ice cream on the bottom, add a few root beer ice cubes, then slowly pour the root beer on top. It will foam a lot, so pour slowly.

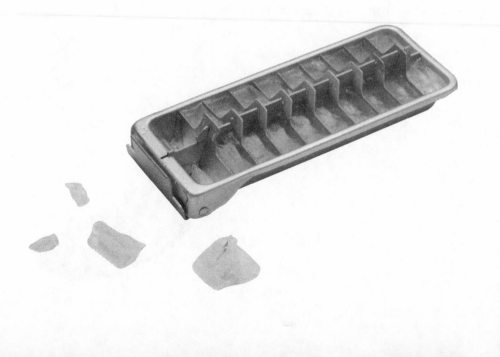

Aunt Audrey's Ice Cream Pie

Chocolate, ice cream, chocolate, pretzels, chocolate, cookies, chocolate . . . yum city.

You will need:

- 2 pints of ice cream (2 flavors that are yummy together)
- Chocolate piecrust (store-bought!)
- 2 cups of chocolate chips or broken-up chocolate bars
- 1 cup of crushed pretzels
- Chocolate cookies

How to:

1. Take the out ice cream out of the freezer and let it soften a bit.

2. Cover the bottom of the piecrust with chocolate chips.

3. Heat the crust in the oven just until the chocolate melts. Remove and let it cool.

4. When the ice cream is just soft enough to spread with the back of a spoon, go ahead and spread one flavor of ice cream on top of the chocolate.

5. Toss a layer of pretzels and extra chocolate over the ice cream.

6. Spread the second layer of ice cream over the pretzels and chocolate.

7. Decorate the top with cookies.

8. Freeze for 2 hours. Take the pie out 15 minutes before serving so it will be easy to cut!

Time Capsule Party

Every decade has a quintessential style. Here's your chance to party in the decade you wish you'd grown up in.

The Vibe

For invitations, make fake concert flyers from photocopies of old CD covers (or vinyl LPs, if you can find them) with your party info!

Dress Code

- **The 50s:** *I Love Lucy* . . . poodle skirts . . . prom dresses and corsages (for guys, denim and pompadours)
- **The 60s:** Woodstock . . . tie-dyes and flower children . . . the Beatles (for guys, peace signs, ponytails, and Afros)
- **The 70s:** Disco . . . Farrah hair . . . halters and short-shorts . . . *Charlie's Angels,* the TV show (for guys, leisure suits and polyester)
- **The 80s:** New Wave . . . Punk Rock . . . Preppies (for guys, faux-Mohawks and skinny ties)
- **The 90s:** Grunge or Glam (for guys, flannels or black nail polish)

Time Capsule

You'll never forget this time in your life, but just in case . . .

- Gather a big box and ask each guest to bring one small item that represents him or her or that is very timely.
- Make a group questionnaire and have each guest answer one question and sign his or her name. Ask questions like "What CD is in your stereo right now?"; "Who is your worst/best teacher?"; and "What's your favorite thing to wear?"
- Include a CD you've burned with recent hits . . . a celebrity magazine . . . a group photo of the party.
- Label the box with the current date and the date you decide your capsule should be opened.

Party Favors

Funny old tapes and CDs • Concert pins • Pet rocks • Rubik's Cubes

Music

- **The 50s:** Frank Sinatra
- **The 60s:** The Rolling Stones
- **The 70s:** Fleetwood Mac
- **The 80s:** The Police
- **The 90s:** Nirvana

Time Capsule Munchies

- **The 50s:** Authentic Onion Dip-a-rama
- **The 60s:** Hippie-Dippie Granola 'n' Oatmeal Chocolate Chip Cookies
- **The 70s:** Cheesy Fondue
- **The 50s meet the 80s:** Strawberry Sorbet Jell-O Ring-a-Ding

Authentic Onion Dip-a-rama

A huge party hit in the 1950s, this snack deserves some modern recognition! (Note: brush and rinse after this one!)

You will need:
- 1 packet of onion soup mix
- 1½ cups of sour cream
- ½ cup of mayonnaise
- ⅓ cup of grated cheese of your choice
- 1 teaspoon of steak sauce

How to:
1. Mix all the ingredients together in a cute serving bowl and chill for at least 2 hours in the fridge.
2. Serve with crackers and cut-up veggies like carrots, cucumbers, and bell peppers.

Hippie-Dippie Granola 'n' Oatmeal Chocolate Chip Cookies

Inspired by granola-eating flower children. Don't be fooled by the healthy ingredients. These cookies are totally decadent and tasta-riffic!

You will need:

- 1 cup of unsalted butter, softened
- 1 cup of brown sugar
- 1 cup of white sugar
- 2 teaspoons of vanilla
- 2 tablespoons of milk
- 2 eggs, beaten
- 2 cups of all-purpose flour
- 1 teaspoon of salt
- 1 teaspoon of baking soda
- 1 teaspoon of baking powder
- 2 ½ cups of old-fashioned oatmeal (not instant)
- ½ cup of granola or granola-style cereal
- 12 ounces of semisweet chocolate chips

How to:

1. Preheat the oven to 350 degrees.

2. Mix the butter, brown sugar, and white sugar with a mixer or by hand.

3. Add the vanilla, milk, and beaten eggs until creamed (blended smoothly).

4. Add the flour, salt, baking soda, and baking powder, and mix until blended.

5. Stir in the oats, granola, and chocolate chips.

6. Drop small spoon-sized scoops of cookie dough about 1 ½ inches apart from each other on a greased cookie sheet.

7. Bake for 10 to 12 minutes or until the cookies are lightly browned.

Cheesy Fondue

Fondue parties were all the rage in the cheesy, swinging 70s—in between dancing the Hustle and doing the Bus Stop, that is.

You will need:

- A fondue pot (Borrow one from family or friends. You can also find them at trendy discount shops.)
- 1 tablespoon of olive oil
- ½ pound of cheddar cheese
- ½ pound of Swiss cheese
- 2 tablespoons of flour
- 2 tablespoons of milk
- ½ tablespoon of garlic powder
- Dashes of salt and pepper
- 1 large loaf of French bread, cubed

How to:

1. Rub olive oil all around the inside of the fondue pot.

2. Grate both cheeses.

3. Mix the cheeses with the flour in a bowl.

4. Pour the milk into the fondue pot and start warming it.

5. Spoon the cheese mixture slowly into the pot and stir constantly until all the cheese is melted.

6. Add the garlic powder, salt, and pepper.

7. Spear the bread cubes with fondue forks, dip, and enjoy!

 *Gruyère is a great Swiss cheese to use.*

Strawberry Sorbet Jell-O Ring-a-Ding

Sorbet is very 1980s, and Jell-O molds were a 50s party staple. Maybe they still are at your grandma's house (shhh, we won't tell).

You will need:

- 2 cups of boiling water
- 2 boxes of strawberry Jell-O
- 1 pint of strawberry sorbet
- 2 pints of strawberries (washed and sliced)
- A dessert ring mold

How to:

1. Boil the water in a teakettle.

2. Empty both packages of Jell-O into a large mixing bowl. Add the boiled water. Stir until the Jell-O dissolves.

3. Add the sorbet and mix until it has melted.

4. Stir in the sliced strawberries.

5. Pour the mixture into the mold and refrigerate overnight or until firm.

6. Release the firm Jell-O onto a large plate or cake stand.

7. Keep your Jell-O Ring-a-Ding in the fridge until party time!

Hawaiian Luau

Host a fun-loving tropical fiesta for a guaranteed good time. Here's how.

The Tropical Vibe

- Peel the labels off fruit cans, back them with cardboard, and use them as invitations (do your mom a favor and relabel your label-less cans).
- Fill a kiddie pool with blue balloons.
- String lanterns and Christmas lights.
- Hang beach towels on the walls or over the food table.
- Get a pink flamingo for a centerpiece.
- Fill a small spray bottle with suntan oil, label it *Summer in a Bottle,* and spritz behind guests' ears to get them in the surf spirit!

Dress Code

No one gets into the party unless they are sporting Hawaiian shirts, surf shorts, or bathing suits. For aloha-challenged friends, make sure to have some plastic leis and grass skirts on hand.

Music

- The Ventures (They recorded the hit version of the *Hawaii Five-O* TV show theme song.)
- The Beach Boys
- The Go-Go's
- Don Ho

Inspirational Movies

- *A Very Brady Sequel*
- *Beach Blanket Bingo*
- *Blue Hawaii*
- *The Endless Summer*
- Gidget movies

Surf's Up Grub

- Pu Pu Platter
- Egg Rolls with Spicy Duck Sauce
- Fruity Yogurt Dip
- Easy Tropical Brownies
- Frosty Mock Mai Tai Punch

Pu Pu Platter (a.k.a. mini–hot dog and pineapple skewers!)

Those TV cooking shows will have nothing on you when you whip up this yummy snack.

You will need:

- 2 packages of hot dogs, turkey franks, or veggie dogs
- Barbecue sauce
- Nonstick spray
- Wooden skewers
- Two 8-ounce cans of pineapple chunks, drained
- Mustard

How to:

1. Cut the hot dogs into thirds.

2. Toss the hot dogs in a bowl and coat them with barbecue sauce.

3. Spray a baking sheet with the nonstick spray and place the hot dog pieces on the sheet.

4. Bake at 350 degrees about 15 minutes, until the hot dogs are bubbly.

5. When the hot dogs cool, place 1 hot dog on each skewer, sandwiched between 2 pineapple chunks.

6. Serve with a hot and spicy mustard on the side.

 Stick the skewers into a pineapple for high drama and a yummy centerpiece. A cheaper alternative? Use half a head of red cabbage instead of the pineapple.

Egg Rolls with Spicy Duck Sauce

Okay, these couldn't be easier (unless you ordered in, but then you'd need a menu and money to tip the delivery guy).

You will need:

- One 12-ounce jar of duck sauce
- One 8-ounce can of crushed pineapple, drained
- 1 teaspoon of hot sauce
- Frozen egg rolls

How to:

1. Mix the duck sauce, pineapple, and hot sauce in a bowl.

2. Cook the egg rolls according to the instructions.

3. Serve the egg rolls hot with the sauce on the side.

Fruity Yogurt Dip

Healthy and great-tasting! Serve with a fruit tray.

You will need the following to make the dip:

• One 8-ounce carton of fruit-flavored yogurt

• 1 cup of frozen dessert topping, thawed

• 1 tablespoon of sugar

• 1 teaspoon of vanilla

How to:

Mix the ingredients in a small mixing bowl until creamy. Refrigerate until serving time.

You will need the following to make a fruit tray:

• Bananas, peeled and cut into chunks

• Oranges, peeled and cut into wedges

• 1 bunch of seedless grapes

• Kiwi (if in season), peeled and sliced

• 1 pint of strawberries

• 1 can of mandarin orange slices, drained

How to serve:

Put the yogurt dip into a small dish in the center of a large plate or tray. Surround the dip with the fruit, arranging it so it looks festive. Provide toothpicks for dipping.

Easy Tropical Brownies

Is there a person alive who doesn't love brownies? Nope, didn't think so.

You will need:

• 1 box of brownie mix (Check the directions to see what ingredients it calls for.)

How to:

Follow the directions on the box to make the brownies. Mix the following into the batter just before you put it in the pan:

• ½ cup of chopped walnuts

• ½ cup of shredded coconut

Garnish the top with extra shredded coconut and bake according to the instructions on the box.

Frosty Mock Mai Tai Punch

Quench your thirst the tropical way.

You will need:

• One 2-liter bottle of ginger ale

• One 2-liter bottle of fruit punch

• 1 large can of pineapple juice

• ½ gallon sherbet (your favorite fruit flavor)

• 2 oranges (peeled and cut into wedges)

How to:

Mix the ginger ale, fruit punch, and pineapple juice in a large punch bowl. When your guests arrive, add the sherbet and fruit. Watch as the sherbet melts and becomes a tropical, frosty frenzy! Serves 14 to 16.

Picnic for Two

In your backyard or at the park, isn't a picnic with your crush the ultimate afternoon activity?

The Vibe

- Think of this day as a chill getaway (even if it's just for a few hours and you're in the backyard).
- Invite your crush/boyfriend to "have lunch under a big blanket of blue sky and hang out on pillows of yellow daisies while birds sing love songs!" Or if that's way too mushy, just ask him to swing by and pick you up for a surprise!

Packing the Picnic Basket

- A little prepicnic prep in the kitchen will make a big impression on your guy (and his stomach).
- Bring a plastic vase for your fresh-picked flowers.
- Wrap real silverware in cloth napkins and tie with ribbon.
- Bring a vintage tablecloth, a blanket, or a sheet for an instant dining room.
- Surprise him with boy toys . . . a football, a Frisbee, and sports magazines.
- Bring an instant camera and bond over the goofy faces you make together.
- Don't forget a trash bag . . . leave only footprints behind!

Rain Date!

If it rains, move the picnic indoors and rent these ultraromantic movies:

- *Pretty Woman*
- *Roman Holiday*
- *Sixteen Candles*

 If you're flying solo (and who hasn't?) and don't have a crush to invite, grab a girlfriend and stake out the park where all the cuties practice baseball. Make sure you bring extra food and boy magnets like a ball or a Frisbee. A dog helps too! Trust us, you won't be alone for long! Bring trashy, grocery store romance novels—for kicks, try to read parts aloud without laughing! Pick flowers and make daisy crowns!

Menu for Two

- Ham 'n' Cheese Croissant Bakes
- Dill-licious Pickles
- Easy Chocolate Mousse

Ham 'n' Cheese Croissant Bakes

With meals this easy, you never have to go hungry again.

You will need:
- ¼ pound of sliced ham
- 2 ounces of cream cheese
- One package of refrigerated crescent roll dough

How to:
1. Preheat the oven to 375 degrees.

2. Chop the ham into small pieces.

3. In a small mixing bowl, blend the ham into the cream cheese.

4. Open the crescent roll package and separate the rolls.

5. Put a spoonful of cream cheese mixture in the center of the triangle and roll it up according to the directions on the package. Make sure the cheese doesn't ooze out the sides.

6. Place the crescent rolls on a greased baking sheet.

7. Bake for 10 to 12 minutes until golden brown.

8. Cool and serve at room temperature.

A Very Veggie Option

Spinach 'n' Cheese Croissant Bakes

Substitute a package of frozen spinach for the ham. Cook and drain it first according to the package instructions. Let it cool before you blend it into the cream cheese.

Dill-licous Pickles

Ever thought of where pickles come from? They don't just grow on trees, you know. They start as cucumbers, and it's up to you to pickle 'em just right!

You will need:

- 5 cups of water
- 1 ¼ cups of white vinegar
- ½ cup of sugar
- ¼ cup of salt
- 1 clove of garlic (peeled, not chopped)
- 1 large sliced onion
- A bunch of fresh dill
- ½ tablespoon of pickling spice
- 3 pounds of Kirby cucumbers (cut lengthwise and in quarters)
- A large glass jar with a lid

How to:

1. Boil the water, vinegar, sugar, and salt together in a pot.

2. Place the garlic, sliced onion, dill sprigs, pickling spice, and quartered cucumbers in the glass container, packing the cucumbers tightly.

3. Pour the cooked mixture into the container with the cucumbers.

4. Cover and refrigerate for at least a day. In this time, the cucumbers will officially graduate into delicious pickles.

Quickie Pickles!

We have a friend, Maia, who cheats a little and just adds quartered cucumbers to pickle juice left over from store-bought pickles. She swears they're just as good! You still have to let them pickle for a day in the fridge!

Easy Chocolate Mousse

Easy! Chocolate! Need we say more?

You will need:

- 1 box of instant chocolate pudding
- Milk
- Whipped topping
- ½ cup of chocolate chips
- 2 individual serving–sized plastic containers with lids

How to:

1. Prepare the pudding according to the instructions on the box, using the milk.

2. Chill the pudding in a bowl in the fridge for at least ½ hour.

3. Gently blend the whipped topping into the pudding, reserving some for garnish, and mix in the chocolate chips.

4. Spoon the mousse into the 2 containers, filling containers ¾ of the way. Fill the rest of the containers with reserved whipped topping before putting the lids on. Store your picnic mousse in the fridge until you're off to the park.

Save leftover mousse in the fridge as a treat for your family. Flavor experiment: Try banana pudding and crumbled vanilla wafers!

Surprise your picnic date: label the container with a homemade label that has both your names on it.

Ali Smith

Best friends **DARREN GREENBLATT** and **ELA JAYNES** make it their business to know everything about fashion, style, and making the world around them a cooler, hipper, and happier place to be. Visit them at www.planetyumthing.net.